Tax processes for businesses

Revision workbook

Teresa Clarke FMAAT

Tax processes for businesses

Revision workbook

Published in 2023 for the Q2022 AAT exam, based on the Finance Act 2021.

This has been written as a revision aid to help you with your studies. It does not replace your study materials and books.

You will need the reference material provided by AAT.

Teresa Clarke FMAAT

CONTENTS

Chapter 1 – Introduction

Chapter 2 – Calculating VAT

Chapter 3 – Registration and de-registration

Chapter 4 – Tax points

Chapter 5 – VAT invoices

Chapter 6 – Input and output tax

Chapter 7 – The VAT return

Chapter 8 – Adjustments, errors and penalties

Chapter 9 - Payroll

Chapter 10 -Tasks to complete

Chapter 11 - Answers

Chapter 1 – Introduction

VAT is an indirect tax on consumer spending and most goods and services supplied within the UK are subject to VAT. VAT registered businesses collect the VAT on behalf of HMRC.

A registered business, or trader, charges VAT on its sales, known as output tax. Tip: Sales go <u>out</u> of the business, so VAT on sales is <u>output</u> tax.

If the customer is also VAT registered, they claim this VAT back from HMRC. Tip: Purchases come <u>in</u>to the business, so VAT on purchases is <u>input</u> tax.

It is the final consumer, who is not VAT registered and cannot reclaim the VAT, that ultimately pays it.

A business which is VAT registered, or should be registered, is known as a <u>taxable person</u>. By this we mean taxable entity, not actually a person.

This workbook will take you through some of the tricky bits in this unit. I hope it helps with your understanding of this topic.

If you are studying for your AAT Level 3 qualification, be sure to use the reference material available from AAT, as this will also be available to you in the exam.

All thresholds and rules mentioned in this book are taken from the Finance Act 2021, so check that this is accurate for the qualification you are studying.

Tax processes for business revision workbook

Chapter 2 – Calculating VAT

Taxable supplies mean taxable sales. The VAT on taxable supplies is charged at one of three different rates.

0% - zero rate,

5% - reduced rate,

20% - standard rate.

To calculate the gross amount of an invoice, or the total of the invoice, we take the net amount and add the VAT at the appropriate rate.

Example

Alexandra runs a furniture shop. She sells a table and chairs set for £960 including VAT at standard rate.

The invoice needs to show the net amount, the VAT and the total or gross amount.

The maths:

Please remember that if you are already confident with the maths and you are getting the correct answers, you don't need to change your method. Any method is correct if it gets the correct answer!

The net amount is 100%

The VAT rate is 20%

The total is 120%

Net amount (before VAT)	100%	
VAT	20%	
Gross amount (inc. VAT)	120%	

In this question we know that the gross amount, or total invoice is £960.00, so we put that in the table first.

5

Net amount (before VAT)	100%	
VAT	20%	
Gross amount (inc. VAT)	120%	£960.00

We know that £960 = 120%, so let's find 1%.

£960.00 / 120 = £8

1% = £8

Now let's fill in the rest of the table by multiplying up by the percentage shown in the table.

Net amount (before VAT)	100%	£800.00 [£8 x 100]
VAT	20%	£160.00 [£8 x 20]
Gross amount (inc. VAT)	120%	£960.00

It doesn't matter which number you know; you can complete the table to find the missing numbers.

The invoice will be detailed using these figures.

Net amount   £800.00
Plus VAT at 20%   £160.00
Total invoice   £960.00

Task 1 in chapter 10 will give you some practice questions for this. You might like to try these now. Alternatively, you can work through the book first.

When calculating VAT in a question, be careful to read the question carefully as it may ask for VAT to be calculated at any of the taxable rates: zero - 0%, reduced - 5% or standard 20%.

If a task mentions exempt supplies, these are outside the scope of VAT. A business cannot register for VAT if it only makes exempt supplies, or sales, as these are not taxable supplies.

The method to calculate VAT at the zero or reduced rate is very similar to the method we used earlier.

Example

Reduced rate:
Tom sells heating oil to customers for use in central heating boilers. The VAT on this type of supply is charged at 5%, the reduced rate. He quotes a customer £500 plus VAT for their oil. This is the net amount.

Net amount (before VAT)	100%	£500.00
VAT	5%	
Gross amount (inc. VAT)	105%	

The net amount is 100%, so we can divide this by the 100 and then multiply by 5%.
£500 / 100 = £5
£5 = 1%
£5 x 5 = £25
This is the VAT amount.

£500 / 100 = £5
£5 x 105 = £525.
This is the VAT inclusive amount, or gross amount.

We can put those figures into a similar table:

Net amount (before VAT)	100%	£500.00
VAT	5%	£25.00
Gross amount (inc. VAT)	105%	£525.00

Zero rate:

This does seem odd because it is zero, but it is still a taxable supply. Do not confuse this with an exempt supply.

A sale of children's clothing of £20 at zero rate would be simply shown like this:

Net amount (before VAT)	100%	£20
VAT	0%	£0
Gross amount (inc. VAT)	100%	£20

Task 2 will give you further examples to practice.

Chapter 3 – Registration and de-registration

A business must register for VAT if its taxable turnover exceeds the current threshold for registration.

A business can voluntarily register for VAT if it makes some taxable supplies.

A business who sells only exempt supplies cannot register for VAT.

The historic test:

If a business exceeds the threshold for taxable supplies over the past 12 months, it must register for VAT within 30 days.

This means when the turnover or sales exceed the limit.

This is not an accounting year, but the last 12 months. This is a rolling 12 month period.

Example of the rolling 12 months

I would check at the end of February 2023 by checking the turnover for the 12 months from 1 March 2022 to 28 February 2023.

I would check at the end of March 2023 by checking the turnover for the 12 months from 1 April 2022 to 31 March 2023.

If I checked the turnover of a business on 31 March 2023 and found that the turnover (sales) was over the threshold, I would need to notify HMRC by 30 April 2023 and my VAT registration would start from 1 May 2023.

Example

Rachael is checking her turnover to see if she needs to register for VAT.

Today's date is 30 April 2023.

Her turnover or sales for the 12 months from 1 May 2022 to 30 April 2023 has exceeded the threshold.

This means she must notify HMRC within 30 days, so by 31 May 2023 and she will need to be registered from 1 June 2023.

The future test:

If a business knows that it will be exceeding the threshold within the next 30 days, it must register immediately.

Example

Serif has started a new business and expects her turnover to be £95,000 in the first month. As she knows that her turnover will exceed the threshold, she must notify HMRC within 30 days, but her registration will start immediately.

There is one exception to this rule. If a business usually has a turnover of £6,000 a month (which would work out at less than the threshold over the full 12 months), but undertakes a one-off job for £30,000 this month, they do not have to register for VAT if they are confident that this is not going to happen again.

Remember:

The historic test is looking at the previous 12 months to see if the threshold has been exceeded. If it has, the business must notify HMRC within 30 days and will be registered on the first day of the following month.

The future test is looking at the next 30 days to see if the threshold is likely to be exceeded. If it is likely, the business must notify HMRC within 30 days, but must be registered straight away. (I know this sounds odd, but basically, they need to be registered from first of the month they know they are going to exceed the threshold).

Task 3 gives you some scenario questions to cover this topic.

De-registration means when a business stops being registered for VAT.

A business must de-register if it stops making taxable supplies.

A business can voluntarily de-register for VAT if it can show that the threshold for the next 12 months will not exceed the registration threshold.

The de-registration threshold is always lower than the registration threshold. It is currently £83,000.

Examples

A business who makes only exempt supplies must de-register from VAT.

A business who makes a mix of taxable and exempt supplies, even if the taxable supplies are below the threshold, can chose to remain registered.

A business which ceases to make any supplies must de-register from VAT.

A business with an expected turnover for the next 12 months of less than the registration threshold can choose to de-register.

A business who makes only zero-rated supplies can remain registered even if their turnover is below the registration limit because these are taxable supplies.

Chapter 4 – Tax points

The VAT tax point is the date when the VAT liability arises. It is the date that the sale or supply is recorded for VAT accounting purposes. It is sometimes seen on documents as the time of supply.

We start with a basic tax point which is the point at which the sale takes place. I refer to sale, but this could also be a service.

If a sale is made on 1 May 2023 this is the basic tax point. The date on which the customer bought the goods.

The actual tax point can change this date.

If payment is received before the basic tax point, then the payment date is the actual tax point.

If the invoice was issued before the sale took place, then the invoice date is the actual tax point.

If the invoice is issued within 14 days of the basic tax point, then this is used as the actual tax point (14-day rule).

This is a difficult topic to master, so I will explain it in with a few examples below.

Example 1

Tahira sells a sofa from her shop on 20 January 2023. The customer pays for the sofa on 20 January 2023. The invoice is raised on 25 January 2023. The sofa is delivered on 12 February 2023.

We look at the first date. 20 January payment was received so this is the basic tax point. However, the invoice was raised within 14 days so we can use the 14-day rule, and the actual tax point will be 25 January.

Example 2

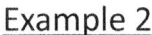

Donna receives an order for a new car from her showroom on 1 March 2023. The car is delivered on 1 April 2023. She pays for it on 18 April 2023. The invoice is raised on 28 April 2023.

The order date is always irrelevant. The first date here is the 1 April, when the car was delivered. The payment was made on 18 April. The invoice was not raised within 14 days. The actual tax point is 1 April.

Example 3

Tom dispatches goods to his customer on 1 July 2023. The invoice is raised on 20 July 2023 and the customer pays for the goods on 25 July 2023.

The first date is the dispatch to the customer. This is the same as delivery, so this is the basic tax point. Because the invoice is not raised within 14 days and the customer pays after they have received the goods, the actual tax point is 1 July.

Example 4

Alek sends a proforma invoice to his customer on 1 January 2023. The customer sends payment on 15 January 2023. Alek sends the invoice on 16 January 2023 and dispatches the goods on 18 January 2023.

The proforma invoice is irrelevant. This is only a quote or request for payment. It is not an invoice for VAT purposes.

The first date is 15 January when the customer sends payment. This is the basic tax point. However, the invoice was issues on 16 January, so this becomes the actual tax point because the 14-day rule applies. The dispatch of the goods was later.

Tax processes for business revision workbook

Example 5

Ali receives a deposit from a customer on 18 March 2023. He dispatches the goods on 20 March 2023. He issues an invoice for the full amount on 1 April 2023. The customer pays on 5 April 2023.

When a deposit is involved, we treat the transaction like two invoices.
1. Deposit was received on 18 March, so this is effectively the first tax point.
2. The goods were dispatched on 20 March, so this would be the basic tax point for the balance, but the invoice was issued within 14 days so the actual tax point for the second part of this would be 1 April.

This is a tricky topic to grasp, so just keep practising. There are more examples to practice in task 4 at the back of this book.

Points to note about the 14-day rule

This rule can be varied by HMRC if a business requests it. Some businesses may send all invoices on the last day of the month, so the rule can be amended for this, but must be approved by HMRC first.

The 14-day rule does not apply to invoices for zero rated goods.

In your assessment, you must assume the 14-day rule applies, unless the question specifically tells you otherwise.

Chapter 5 – VAT invoices

All businesses registered for VAT must provide a customer with a VAT invoice within 30 days of the supply of the goods or payment being received. This means physically sending it to them within 30 days. Don't confuse this with the tax point.

There is no set format for a VAT invoice, but it must include certain information. You do not need to memorise this as it will be in your reference material provided in the exam. However, it is a good idea to read this through now to ensure that you understand it.

When calculating VAT on an invoice you should not use normal maths rounding rules, but instead, round down.

For example, if the net amount of an invoice is £31.63, and we calculate the VAT at 20%, the calculator will show £6.326. We round this down to £6.32.

Discounts on invoices

Trade discount is taken off the net amount before the VAT is calculated. This type of discount is often given to builders buying building materials. The building material seller will give the builder a set trade discount to encourage them to buy from their store.

For example, if the net price (often called book price or list price) was £300 and the builder was being given a 10% trade discount, our starting net price would be £270. The VAT would be calculated on the £270.

£300 less trade discount of 10%	= £270
Plus VAT at 20%	= £54
Total invoice	= £324

Bulk discount is treated in the same way as trade discount. It is also taken off before the VAT is calculated.

Sometimes a seller will advertise a promotion or sale as "we will pay the VAT". This is not strictly the case when working out the invoice.

For example, if a seller was advertising new beds to customers and the usual price was £1,200 including VAT and they offered to "pay the VAT", we would first work out what that would be.

£1,200 including VAT = 120%
£1,200 / 120 = £10
£10 = 1%
£10 x 20 = £200
The VAT amount on the original price is £200.

The new price of the bed to the customer is £1,000, but we need to draw up the invoice for this.
£1,000 is the gross amount or total invoice. We need to treat this as the VAT inclusive amount and work backwards to calculate the VAT on this.
£1,000 including VAT = 120%
(£1,000 / 120) x 20 = £166.66 (rounded down)

The invoice to be entered for the sale will be:
Net amount   £833.34
VAT at 20%   £166.66
Total invoice   £1,000.00

Make sure you understand this before moving on.

Prompt payment discount is offered to customers if they settle or pay their invoices within a certain period, say 7 days. The invoice is issued in the normal way and then a credit note issued if the customer takes advantage of the prompt payment discount.

The invoice might be for £200 plus VAT of £40, with a total of £240 owing. If they are offered a prompt payment discount of 5% if they pay quickly, they need only pay £228 including VAT. The business would then issue a credit note for the difference.

Invoice
Net amount   £200.00
VAT at 20%   £ 40.00
Total due   £240.00

Discount of 5% given if payment made within 7 days.

The customer pays within 7 days and sends a payment of £228.00.

Credit note
Net amount   £10.00
VAT at 20%   £ 2.00
Total credit   £12.00

The amount invoiced of £240, less the credit note of £12, equals the £228 received.

Task 5 gives you more practice with VAT invoices.

Chapter 6 – Input and output tax

Input tax is VAT on purchases or other expenses bought by the business. Output tax is VAT on sales made by the business.

Generally, a VAT registered business will reclaim input tax on their purchases and other expenses, but some items are not allowed, known as blocked. You will find more information about this in your reference material.

Input VAT on most forms of business entertaining is blocked. The exception to this is when the entertaining is for the employees, or customers from overseas. These are allowed, so the VAT can be reclaimed.

Input VAT on the purchase of cars is blocked. The exception to this is when the cars are 100% for business use, such as taxis, pool cars and driving instructor cars. Do not confuse this with commercial vehicles, such as vans and lorries, where all the VAT is reclaimable.

Task 6 gives you some practice on these types of questions.

Fuel scale charge

When it comes to the running expenses of the car, such as the fuel and maintenance, there is a scheme which allows the business to reclaim the VAT, even though it may be used for both business and personal journeys. This is called the fuel scale charge.

The fuel scale charge is an extra output tax that the business can pay to HMRC to claim all the running expenses of a car. The fuel scale charges are provided by HMRC and vary depending on the emissions of the car. You will be provided with these figures in your exam; check your reference material.

Example

Jodie uses her car for both business and private journeys. The emissions of her car are 201g per km (201g/km). The fuel scale charge for emissions of 200g/km is:

VAT inclusive charge £438.00
Output VAT charge £73.00

This is because we round down to the nearest g/km, so 201g/km is rounded down to 200g/km.

The output tax charge is the figure we need for our VAT return.

This figure of £73 is added to the output tax, the amount payable to HMRC. We pay this to them as a charge, then we can claim back all the input VAT on expenses for the car in that VAT period.

Make sure you understand this before moving on.

When cars, vans and other assets are sold, VAT is charged to the buyer if VAT was reclaimed when the business purchased the non-current asset.

Example

A car was purchased for use as a taxi in 2019 and the VAT was reclaimed from HMRC. The car is sold in 2023, and VAT is charged on the sale.

A car is purchased by the business 2020 to be used in the business and for private use, so no VAT is reclaimed. The car is sold in 2023 and no VAT is charged on the sale.

Task 7 provides some practice calculations.

Some businesses will sell goods at standard rate, reduced rate or zero rate, and some will sell goods which are exempt from VAT. There will be others which sell a mix of standard rated goods and exempt goods. This is called a partially exempt trader, as they are partially exempt from VAT.

The business will charge some goods plus VAT at 20% (standard rated) and some goods with no VAT (exempt).

The business can reclaim VAT on all purchases that relate to the standard rate sales.

The business cannot reclaim VAT on purchases that relate to the exempt sales.

The expenses or overheads that cannot be allocated directly to either sale are known as mixed supplies and are treated differently.

Example

Aleksandra owns a house which she lets out to tenants. This is an exempt supply. This means that she does not charge VAT to her tenants.

Aleksandra also owns a building business where she builds conservatories and garden rooms for customers. This is a standard rated supply, so she charges VAT to her customers.

When Aleksandra spends money on the tenanted house for a new carpet, she cannot reclaim the VAT because the supply or sale is exempt.

When Aleksandra spends money providing flooring in a garden room for a customer, she can reclaim the VAT because the supply or sale is standard rate.

When Aleksandra spends money on her mobile phone, which she uses for both businesses, she can claim some of this input tax back. This is based on a percentage of the sales made for both the exempt and standard supplies. So, if 20% of her sales were from the house rent and 80% from building garden rooms, she would reclaim 80% of the mixed VAT.

HOWEVER, there is an exception to this rule, and this is called the de minimus limit. There are two tests for this.

Test 1 - If the total input tax is less than the de minimus limit of £625 per month, then it can all be reclaimed.

Test 2 – If the input tax on the taxable supplies is less that the de minimus limit of £625 per month and the total exempt supplies are less than 50% of the total supplies, all the input VAT can be reclaimed.

Aleksandra's sales for the quarter ending 31 March 2023 are shown below.

Taxable supplies (building work carried out) during the quarter were £80,000.
Exempt supplies (rental income) during the quarter were £3,600.

Input VAT relating to taxable supplies was £7,000.
Input VAT relating to exempt supplies was £800.
Input VAT relating to mixed supplies or other expenses was £1,000.

The input VAT on the taxable supplies can all be reclaimed.

The input VAT on the exempt supplies cannot be reclaimed unless the total input tax is less than £625 OR the input tax on the taxable supplies is less than the £625 and the total exempt supplies are less than 50% of the total supplies.

Test 1: The total input tax is £8,800 [£7,000 + £800 + £1,000]. When we divide this by the 3 months in the quarter, this is more than £625 per month, so the full input tax cannot be reclaimed using this rule.

Test 2: Looking at the second test, we can see that the input tax relating to the taxable supplies is £7,000. This is still more than £625.

The input VAT relating to the mixed supplies can only be partly reclaimed.

Standard rate supplies (sales) £80,000 divided by total sales £83,600 will give the percentage of the mixed supply input VAT that can be reclaimed.

(80,000/83,600) x 100 = 95.7%.

The mixed VAT amount is £1,000, so 95.7% of this can be reclaimed.

Aleksandra can reclaim the VAT on the taxable supplies of £7,000, plus £957 of the mixed VAT.

This may seem quite complicated, but it is good to understand. Your AAT questions will not usually ask for the full calculation, but it is always good to fully understand what you are doing. The exam style question is more likely to ask whether the de minimus rule applies or not.

Tasks 8 and 9 give practice on this topic.

Chapter 7 – The VAT return

The VAT return is generally submitted online. It will something like this, but most businesses who will be submitting their VAT return online using Making Tax Digital will see this in a different format. However, the box numbers will be the same.

VAT Return 1 Apr 23 to 30 Jun 23		£
VAT due on sales and other outputs	Box 1	1,000.00
VAT due on intra-community acquisitions of goods made in Northern Ireland from EU member states	Box 2	0.00
Total VAT due (the sum of boxes 1 and 2)	Box 3	1,000.00
VAT reclaimed on purchases and other inputs *& Bad debt relief.* (including acquisitions from the EU)	Box 4	600.00
Net VAT to be paid to Customs by you (difference between boxes 3 and 4)	Box 5	400.00
Total value of sales and all other outputs excluding VAT (whole pounds only)	Box 6	5,000
Total value of purchases and all other inputs excluding VAT (whole pounds only)	Box 7	4,000
Total value of intra-community dispatches of goods and related costs, excluding VAT., from Northern Ireland to EU Member States	Box 8	0
Total value of intra-community acquisitions of goods and related costs, excluding VAT, made in Northern Ireland from EU Member States	Box 9	0

You need to be familiar with the VAT return for your level 3 exam. You may be asked to complete a VAT return or, more likely, you may be asked to analyse information or make adjustments or corrections.

Task 10 gives you practice completing a VAT return and task 11 gives you practice with adjustments.

Chapter 8 – Adjustments, errors and penalties

Bad debt relief

When a business pays over the output tax to HMRC, payment may not have been received by the customer by this date. Sometimes a customer does not pay. This is an irrecoverable or bad debt. The VAT already paid to HMRC can be reclaimed. This is called bad debt relief.

There are conditions for a bad debt relief claim.

The debt must be at least 6 months overdue (from the date payment was expected if credit was offered).

The irrecoverable debt must be written off in the accounting records.

Output was actually charged on the sale.

The debt has not been sold on to a debt collecting or factoring company.

The main ones to note here are the 6 months overdue condition and the writing off of the debt in the accounts.

If a bad debts meets all conditions, the VAT paid on the original invoice can be reclaimed as an expense (bad debt expense). VAT on expenses or purchases are entered into box 4, so the bad debt relief is added to this figure.

Example

VAT on purchases (box 4) = £500.00

A bad debt over 6 months old and written off in the accounts totals £600 including VAT. The VAT amount is £100. This is added to box 4.

VAT on purchases (box 4) = £600.00 (£500.00 + £100).

Reverse charges

This scheme applies to the building industry and is for businesses who are VAT registered and use the CIS scheme (Construction Industry Scheme). The CIS scheme is not covered in this unit, but you need to be aware of its existence.

If a sub-contract builder sends an invoice to a main contractor, who is also registered under the CIS scheme, he does receive the VAT. The main contractor receiving the invoice, will account for the VAT in their VAT return.

This is best explained in an example.

Example

Paul has been contracted to provide plumbing services to CP Ltd, who build garden rooms for the public.

Paul sends his invoice to CP Ltd for £1,300 plus VAT of £260. He puts a note on the invoice explaining that the domestic reverse charge applies.

CP Ltd send Paul his payment of £1,300 (no VAT paid).

Paul completes his VAT return by entering the net amount of the sales invoice of £1,300 in box 6, as normal.

CP Ltd complete their VAT return by entering the £260 in both boxes 1 and 4, thereby charging it to themselves and claiming it back (essentially cancelling each other out) and show the net amount of £1,300 in both boxes 6 (net sales) box 7 (net purchases).

Dealing with errors

If a business makes an error in a VAT return this must be corrected as soon as possible. If an error or mistake is careless or deliberate, then the business may receive a penalty. The penalty is based on a percentage of the net error.

If a business finds an error that is not deliberate, and is a genuine mistake, the penalty would be between 0% and 30% if voluntarily declared. If HMRC find the error, this could be between 15% and 30%.

You do **NOT** need to remember these percentages in the AAT level 3 exam as this information is in the reference material.

For deliberate errors voluntarily declared the penalty is between 20% and 70%. If HMRC find the error this is between 35% and 70%.

For concealed errors voluntarily declared the penalty is between 30% and 100%. If HMRC find the error this is between 50% and 100%.

If a business fails to submit the actual VAT return, HMRC may issue an assessment of what they believe is due and this must be paid by the business.

Not all errors need to be declared to HMRC. If they fall into the following categories, they can be declared on the next VAT return. This information is given in the AAT exam reference material, so you do **NOT** need to remember it.

The net error is no more than £10,000 or between £10,000 and £50,000, but no more than 1% of the box 6 figure.

Errors must be declared, or disclosed, to HMRC if they are above £50,000, over £10,000 and more than 1% of the box 6 figure, if they are deliberate or if they are older than 4 years.

Task 12 gives some practice on errors.

Failure to register

If a trader fails to register for VAT when they have exceeded the threshold, they will need to account for the VAT that should have been charged to customers from the date they should have registered.

If a business exceeded the threshold in February, they should register by the end of March and start accounting for VAT from 1 April. If they fail to do this, they are liable for the VAT that should have been charged from 1 April. They may also be charged a penalty.

If a business should have registered for VAT and needs to pay the amount, they should have paid to HMRC, they can treat this in two ways.

Example

The business issued invoices to customers totalling £40,000 but did not register for VAT when they should have done. No VAT was charged to the customers.

The VAT that should have been charged would be £40,000 x 20% = £8,000. The trader can pay this full amount over to HMRC using the VAT exclusive method.

Alternatively, they can treat the £40,000 as a VAT inclusive amount. (£40,000 / 120) x 20 = £6,666.66 (rounded down for VAT!)

The second option costs the trader less is and usually the option a business will choose.

However, if the trader is issuing invoices to VAT registered customers, who claim the VAT back, they can ask them to pay the full £8,000. The customer does not have to do this but may choose to do so to keep business relationships good.

Your AAT reference material provides information on this topic, so you can refer to this in your exam too.

Chapter 9 – Payroll

Most employers must register for payroll with HMRC. If an employer pays an employee more than £120 a week, pays an employee who has another job, pays an employee who receives a pension, or provides benefits to an employee, they must register. Businesses can register online.

A business must register before the first pay day, but not more than 2 months before the first pay day.

If Jonno is due to be paid on 31 March, the business cannot register before 31 January (2 months) but must register before 31 March.

An employer must keep records including the gross pay, the income tax (PAYE deductions), the National Insurance (NICs) for both employer and employee, plus other deductions made, or benefits given.

All records must be kept for at least 3 years. A penalty of up to £3,000 can be issued if adequate records are not kept.

Statutory deductions are compulsory deductions made from an employee's pay. The main statutory deductions are income tax (PAYE), National Insurance contributions (NICs) and pension contributions. Other deductions are called non-statutory, and these are voluntarily deducted from the employee's pay. The employee chooses to have these deductions taken and could be for charitable donations, known as GAYE, give as you earn.

Task 13 gives practice for payroll topics.

Employers' responsibilities to report

Payslips must be legally provided to employees. They must include the following:
- Gross pay
- Details of deductions
- Net pay after deductions
- Hours worked, if the employee is paid hourly.
- Total of pay and deductions for the current tax year to the current date

The payslip can be in paper format, but many are now electronic. Both are acceptable.

An employer must report information to HMRC using RTI (real time information). This means that the employer must submit the information about pay to HMRC on or before the pay date.

When an employer pays an employee, they must submit an FPS (full payment submission) to HMRC using their online payroll service. This will be done through the employer's payroll software. Again, this must be done on or before the pay date.

A tax month for payroll is from the 6th of a month to the 5th of the following month. For example, the month will start on 6th May 2023 and finish on 5th June 2023.

Check the reference material provided for your exam, as much of this information will be included and available in the exam.

When an employee leaves, the employer must give them a P45. The employee will keep part 1 and hand parts 2 and 3 to their new employer. This will provide information to the new employer including the employee's details, leaving date, tax code, total pay and deductions for the year so far and details of any student loan deductions.

If an employer has not paid any employees in a month, they will submit an EPS (employer payment summary) instead of the FPS. It will contain similar information but will declare that no payments were made to employees during that month.

Payments to HMRC

The employer must pay all deductions to HMRC by the 19th of the month following payment, or 22nd of the month if paid by electronic payment. If the employee was paid on 30 June 2023, the deductions must be paid to HMRC by 19 July 2023. If these are to be paid by electronic payment, they must be paid by 22 July 2023.

Year end

At the end of the tax year, the employer must submit the final FPS and make payment of any outstanding PAYE or NIC deductions. They must complete a P60 for every employee who is still employed at the end of the year (those who have left will have received a P45 instead). This shows the employee's pay for the tax year and the income tax and NICs that have been deducted.

The P11D is also completed at the end of the year. This shows the benefits received by the employee, such as a company car or medical insurance. The employee does not pay NICs on the P11D benefits, but the employer must pay class 1a NICs.

Task 14 gives practice on some of these payroll topics.

Tasks 15 onwards will contain a mix of questions to check your knowledge.

Chapter 10 – Tasks to complete

Task 1

Alexandra has given you the following list of sales made this month, but there are numbers missing. Complete the table below by working out the net, VAT or total amounts. All sales were made at the standard rate of 20%.

Note: Net amount before VAT = VAT exclusive of VAT
        Gross amount after VAT – VAT inclusive of VAT

Invoice number:	Net amount (before VAT)	VAT	Gross amount (after VAT)
001	150.00	30.00	
002	400.00		480.00
003	300.00		
004			312.00
005			840.00
006	60.00		
007		200.00	
008			115.80
009	65.50		
010		11.16	

Task 2

a) Indicate whether the following statements are true or false.

	True	False
A taxable person is a business that is, or should be, registered for VAT.		
Output tax is always charged at 20% by a VAT registered business.		
Reduced rate VAT is charged at 5%.		
A business who sells only exempt supplies are not making taxable supplies.		

b) Complete the missing figures in the table below.

Invoice number:	VAT rate	Net amount (before VAT)	VAT	Gross amount (after VAT)
AB1	20%	35.00		
AB2	5%	26.00		
AB3	20%			118.20
AB4	0%	86.00		
AB5	5%			69.30
AB6	5%		5.10	

Task 3

a) Carys started her business on 1 November 2021. Her monthly taxable turnover is £10,000 per month.

(i) What month does she exceed the current threshold of £85,000?

Workings:

Answer: June / July / August / September

(ii) By what date should she notify HMRC?

Answer: 31 August 2022 / 31 July 2022 / 31 September 2021

(iii) When will her VAT registration start from?

Answer: 1 August 2022 / 1 September 2022 / 31 August 2022

b) Stacey is starting a new business on 1 May 2023 selling agricultural machinery and expects her turnover to be in the region of £250,000 a month. These are all taxable supplies.

What date does Stacey need to register from?

Answer: 1 May 2023 / 31 May 2023 / 1 June 2023

c) Trudy started business on 1 April 2022. Her taxable turnover for the first 6 months was £6,000 a month, then it rose to £10,000 a month.

(i) On what date does Trudy's business exceed the threshold.

Workings:

Answer: December 2022 / January 2023 / February 2023

(ii) By what date should Trudy notify HMRC.

Answer: 31 January 2023 / 28 February 2023 / 31 March 2023

Task 4

Identify the actual tax points in the following examples by ticking the correct box.

Scenario			
Sheena receives payment from a customer on 1 March. She dispatches the goods on 5 March. She issues the invoice on 17 March.	1 March	5 March	15 March
Ferhaan receives payment from a customer on 1 April. He dispatches the goods on 1 May. He issues the invoice on 5 May.	1 April	1 May	5 May
Kaye dispatches goods on 1 July. She issues the invoice on 12 July. She receives payment on 15 August.	1 July	12 July	15 August
Carly receives an order on 1 June. She dispatches the goods on 5 June. She issues the invoice on 6 June and receives payment the same day.	1 June	5 June	6 June
Zenildo issues an invoice to a customer on 2 June. He dispatches the goods on 4 June. He receives payment on 10 June.	2 June	4 June	10 June
Mo receives payment for goods on 1 October. He dispatches goods on 4 October. He issues the invoice on 6 October.	1 October	4 October	6 October

Task 5

a) Complete the following invoices.
   Hint: remember to round down the VAT.

Quantity	Unit price £	Total £
400	3.50	
100	1.27	
50	0.60	
	Total net price	
	VAT at 20%	
	Total invoice	

Quantity	Unit price £	Total £
27	1.21	
33	1.59	
49	2.11	
	Total net price	
	VAT at 20%	
	Total invoice	

b) Alicja issues an invoice for standard rated goods. The list price of the goods was £580 excluding VAT. She offers the customer a trade discount of 10%. How much VAT will be shown on the invoice?

Workings:

Answer:

c) Baiba sells bookcases with a normal selling price of £240. She is running a sale at the moment where she is offering to pay the VAT for the customer. How much VAT will she need to show on her discounted invoice?

Workings:

Answer:

d) True or false?

A business offers a prompt payment discount to its customers if they pay within 7 days. The invoice is sent for the full amount, and a credit note is sent for the discount allowed if the customer takes advantage of the discount and pays within the 7 days.

True / False

Task 6

Calculate the amount of VAT that can be reclaimed on each of the following expenses for a VAT registered trader (business). Remember that some VAT is blocked.

	VAT inclusive amount £	VAT reclaimable £
A delivery van bought to deliver goods to customers.	33,600.00	
A restaurant meal for a UK based customer to thank them for their custom.	264.00	
A car purchased for use by the employees and kept on the work premises when not in use (pool car).	19,200.00	
A Christmas party where the employees each bring a guest, meaning half are employees and half are not.	984.00	
A hotel and meal for a customer visiting from China to discuss future work.	228.00	
A car purchased for use by the director, with mixed personal and business use.	25,200.00	
Stationery for use in the office at the head office.	105.60	

Task 7

a) Cathy purchases a car for use in her business, which she intends to use for private journeys at the weekends.

(i) Can she reclaim VAT on the purchase cost of the vehicle?

YES / NO

(ii) If Cathy pays the fuel scale charge, can she reclaim the VAT on the running costs of the car?

YES / NO

b) Complete the table below to show whether output tax should be charged on the sale of the following non-current assets.

Non-current asset	Input tax reclaimed on original purchase	Sale price excluding VAT	Output tax to be charged on sale
Delivery van	Yes	13,500.00	
Car	No	6,000.00	
Machinery	Yes	14,000.00	

Task 8

Trudy's business makes both taxable and exempt supplies (sales). She uses the partial exemption scheme to calculate the VAT she can reclaim on her purchases.

Trudy has provided you with the following information.

Taxable supplies for the quarter	£28,000
Exempt supplies for the quarter	£8,000

Input VAT for taxable supplies	£700
Input VAT for exempt supplies	£500
Input VAT for other expenses	£300

Calculate how much input tax can be reclaimed this quarter.

Workings:

Answer:

Task 9

Stacey's business makes both taxable and exempt supplies. Details of the business activity for the past quarter is shown below.

Taxable supplies	£70,000
Exempt supplies	£20,000
Input tax on taxable supplies	£1,500
Input tax on exempt supplies	£1,500
Input tax on mixed overheads (expenses)	£1,500

Calculate the amount of input tax that can be reclaimed this quarter.

Workings:

Answer:

Task 10

George operates the standard VAT scheme and submits his VAT returns quarterly. He has provided you with the following information.

	Net £	VAT £	Total £
SDB – standard rated sales	10,000	2,000	12,000
SDB – zero rated sales	5,000	0	5,000
PDB – standard rated purchases	4,000	800	4,800
PDB – zero rated purchases	200	0	200
PRDB – standard rated purchase returns	300	60	360

Complete the VAT return using this information. Be careful to include two decimal places in boxes 1 to 5, and whole pounds in boxes 6 to 9.

VAT Return 1 Jan 23 to 31 Mar 23		£
VAT due on sales and other outputs	Box 1	
VAT due on intra-community acquisitions of goods made in Northern Ireland from EU member states	Box 2	
Total VAT due (the sum of boxes 1 and 2)	Box 3	
VAT reclaimed on purchases and other inputs (including acquisitions from the EU)	Box 4	
Net VAT to be paid to Customs by you (difference between boxes 3 and 4)	Box 5	
Total value of sales and all other outputs excluding VAT (whole pounds only)	Box 6	
Total value of purchases and all other inputs excluding VAT (whole pounds only)	Box 7	
Total value of intra-community dispatches of goods and related costs, excluding VAT., from Northern Ireland to EU Member States	Box 8	
Total value of intra-community acquisitions of goods and related costs, excluding VAT, made in Northern Ireland from EU Member States	Box 9	

Task 11

a) Khan Systems is a small business making only taxable supplies. They have provided you with the following information.

Standard rated sales including VAT	£44,004
Standard rated sales returns including VAT	£3,000
Standard rated purchases including VAT	£12,000
Standard rated purchase returns including VAT	£600
Zero rated purchases	£2,000

Calculate the VAT payable or reclaimable for Khan Systems.

Workings:

Answer: £ _____ payable/reclaimable

b) Prime Ltd has output tax this quarter of £18,000 and input tax of £22,000. Calculate the amount payable to or reclaimable from HMRC.

Answer: £ _____ payable / reclaimable

Task 12

a) Jenny has written off a bad debt in her accounts that is more than 6 months old. The customer owed £3,600 including VAT. Calculate the amount of VAT Jenny can claim as bad debt relief and identify which box she needs to add this to.

Bad debt relief:

Add to Box:

b) Jenny has provided you with information about a net error in her previous VAT return, which was neither careless nor deliberate. Identify whether she can include this in her next VAT return or whether she must make a separate disclosure.

Net error is £11,000
Turnover for the period (box 6 figure) is £90,000

Answer: Include in next VAT return / make a separate disclosure.

c) Regan is completing his VAT return for the quarter and has discovered the following errors in the previous VAT return. All were non-deliberate and non-careless.

The input tax was under-stated by £300.
No input tax was claimed on the purchase of a new machine costing £18,000 including VAT.
Input tax was wrongly claimed on the purchase of a car costing £33,180 including VAT.

Identify the net error and decide whether this can be included in the VAT return or whether a separate disclosure is needed.

Workings:

Net error amount:

Answer: Enter in next VAT return / Separate disclosure required

Task 13

Identify whether the following statements are true or false.

Statement	True	False
An employee can register for payroll up to 6 months before they pay their first employee.		
Payroll records must be kept for a minimum of 2 years.		
Income tax (PAYE) is a statutory deduction.		
Income tax (PAYE) is calculated on net pay.		
A charitable donation is an example of a non-statutory deduction.		
Gross pay, minus deductions equals net pay.		

Task 14

a) RTI is the system which requires all employers to submit their payroll information to HMRC. What does RTI stand for?

Answer:

b) FPS is a report submitted by all employers on or before the pay date giving information about the payments made to, and deduction made from, employees. What does FPS stand for?

Answer:

c) If an employer has not paid any employees during the month, which report must be submitted to HMRC declaring this? Choose the correct option.

FPS / P45 / RTI / EPS / P11D

d) When an employee leaves, the employer must issue them with which of the following? Choose the correct option.

P60 / P45 / P11D

e) Identify whether the following statements are true or false.

Statement	True	False
A P60 contains information about the employee benefits for the year, such as company car.		
An employer does not need to issue a payslip if the gross pay is less than £150.		
The employer will pay NIC class 1a on taxable benefits provided to employees.		
PAYE and NIC deductions must be paid to HMRC by the 22nd of the following month if payments are made electronically.		

Task 15

a) Ollie makes only exempt supplies. His turnover was £90,000 for the past 12 months. Does he need to register for VAT?

Yes / No

b) Roger makes only zero-rated supplies. His turnover was £90,000 for the past 12 months. Does he need to register for VAT?

Yes / No

c) Rusty makes both standard and zero rates supplies. His standard rated supplies for the past 12 months totalled £50,000. His zero-rated supplies for the past 12 months totalled £40,000. Does he need to register for VAT.

Yes / No

d) Mary makes both standard rated and exempt supplies. Her standard rated supplies for the past 12 months totalled £40,000. Her exempt supplies for the past 12 months totalled £90,000. Does she need to register for VAT?

Yes / No

Task 16

a) Carys delivers goods to a customer on 2 April 2023. She issues the invoice on 10 April 2023. The customer pays on 15 April 2023.

What is the tax point?

2 April / 10 April / 15 April

b) Identify whether input tax can be reclaimed on the following purchases/expenses.

Purchase / expense	Reclaimable	Not reclaimable
A car purchased for use as a taxi.		
Food for the Christmas party for employees only.		
A car purchased for use by the director for both business and private journeys.		
Cost of entertaining customers visiting from China.		
Cost of entertaining UK customers at local restaurant.		
A van purchased for use within the business.		

c) Jane has decided to pay the fuel scale charge to reclaim VAT on the running costs of the director's car. The amount payable is £240. To which box of the VAT should this charge be added?

Answer:

d) Jane wishes to claim bad debt relief on two irrecoverable debts. She has provided you with the following information. Identify which VAT period the bad debt relief can be claimed and calculate the amount to be reclaimed. Choose the correct option.

Bad debt inc VAT £	Date payment was due	VAT period in which the bad debt relief can be claimed	Amount of bad debt relief to be reclaimed £
3,600	30 Aug 2022	Quarter ending 31 Mar 2023 Quarter ending 30 Jun 2023 Quarter ending 30 Sept 2023	
540	30 Nov 2022	Quarter ending 31 Mar 2023 Quarter ending 30 Jun 2023 Quarter ending 30 Sept 2023	
1,200	31 Dec 2022	Quarter ending 31 Mar 2023 Quarter ending 30 Jun 2023 Quarter ending 30 Sept 2023	

Task 17

Complete the following table by filling in the missing figures.

Net amount £	VAT rate	VAT amount £	Total £
200.00	20%	40.00	240.00
310.00	5%		325.50
	20%	294.00	1764.00
387.25	20%		
474.63	5%		
2,680.80	0%		
9,761.33	20%		
	20%	1,466.00	
	5%	130.00	

Task 18

Heron Enterprises has calculated the VAT owed to HMRC this quarter as £3,185.95.

It has been noticed that a credit note sent to a supplier for goods returned has not been included in the records. The credit note was for £250 plus VAT.

a) Calculate the VAT amount on the credit note.

Answer:

b) Calculate the adjusted amount payable to HMRC.

Answer:

c) The amount payable to HMRC is shown in which box of the VAT return?

Answer:

Task 19

Monika started her business on 1 April 2022. She makes only standard rated supplies. Her taxable supplies are approximately £15,000 every month.

a) In which month will Monika exceed the threshold for registration?

Workings:

Answer:

b) By what date does Monika need to notify HMRC that she has exceeded the threshold?

Answer:

c) What date will Monika need to start accounting for VAT?

Answer:

Task 20

a) Richard runs a market stall selling fresh vegetables. All his sales are zero-rated, and his turnover is well below the compulsory registration threshold. He chooses to register for VAT. Which of the following might be his reason for voluntarily registering for VAT?

   a. He can start charging VAT on his sales.
   b. He makes only zero-rated purchases.
   c. He makes a mix of zero and standard rated purchases. (He can claim back the VAT on the standard rated purchases).

b) George runs a market stall selling fresh fish. All his sales are zero-rated but his turnover is above the compulsory registration threshold. He has applied to be exempt from registration. Which of the following might be his reason for applying for exemption?

   a. His business makes only zero-rated purchases. (He would have nothing to pay HMRC and nothing to claim back as his purchases are also zero-rated).
   b. He doesn't want to charge VAT to his customers.
   c. His prices will need to increase if he registers.

c) True or false?

If a business makes a mix of standard rated and exempt-rated supplies, it cannot claim back any input tax?

True / False

Task 21

Lang is completing her VAT return for the quarter. She has provided you with the following information, taking from the VAT account.

Output tax   £42,000
Input tax   £14,000

You are also told that no adjustments have been made for the following.

Bad debt relief on an invoice totalling £360.00 including VAT.
Fuel scale charges with a total VAT of £140.

a) What will the entry be for Box 1 of the VAT return?

Workings:

Answer:

b) What will the entry be for Box 4 of the VAT return?

Workings:

Answer:

c) How much VAT is payable due to, or from HMRC?

Answer:

Task 22

Identify whether the following statements are true or false.

Statement	True	False
The amount of pay an employee receives after deductions is called the net pay.		
An employer must register for payroll before the first pay day.		
Mavis employs one part-time employee, but she is a sole trader, so she does not have to register for payroll.		
Net pay = gross pay – employee's NI contribution – income tax.		
Income tax and NICs are compulsory deductions from an employee's pay.		
Employers can send payslips to employees in paper-format only.		
An EPS report is used if the employer has paid employees during the month.		
A P45 is issued by the employer to an employee who is leaving their employment.		
The P11D is completed by an employer for every employee who has received taxable benefits during the year.		
A P60 is given to all employees every time they are paid.		
A tax month for payroll is from the 1st to the 30th or 31st of the month.		

Task 23

Identify whether the following errors can be declared in the next VAT return or whether they need to be separately disclosed to HMRC.

Amount of error £	Turnover for the current period £	Include in next VAT return	Separate disclosure required
4,000	80,000		
14,000	150,000		
52,000	1,500,000		
300	30,000		
8,000	80,000		
28,000	3,000,000		
1,000	50,000		
13,000	90,000		
12,000	1,300,000		
60,000	32,000,000		

Task 24

Justine receives a deposit from a customer on 8 July 2022.

She dispatches the goods on 20 July 2022.

She sends the invoice on 25 July 2022.

She receives the balance of the payment on 28 July 2022.

a) Identify the tax point for the deposit.

Answer:

b) Identify the tax point for the balance of the invoice.

Answer:

Task 25

Shirley is a VAT registered trader. She has provided you with the following information for her VAT return for the quarter ending 31 March 2023.

	Net £	VAT £	Total £
SDB – standard rated sales	47,000.00	9,400.00	56,400.00
SRDB – standard rated sales returns	3,000.00	600.00	3,600.00
PDB – standard rated purchases	12,500.00	2,500.00	15,000.00
PDB – zero rated purchases	800.00	0.00	800.00
PRDB – standard rated purchase returns	600.00	120.00	720.00

You have also been told the following:

A car was purchased for £30,000 including VAT and no entries have been made for this.

An adjustment needs to be made for a bad debt of £4,800 including VAT.

Complete the VAT return on the next page using this information.

Workings:
Box 1
Box 2
Box 3
Box 4
Box 5
Box 6
Box 7
Box 8
Box 9 .

VAT Return 1 Jan 23 to 31 Mar 23		£
VAT due on sales and other outputs	Box 1	
VAT due on intra-community acquisitions of goods made in Northern Ireland from EU member states	Box 2	
Total VAT due (the sum of boxes 1 and 2)	Box 3	
VAT reclaimed on purchases and other inputs (including acquisitions from the EU)	Box 4	
Net VAT to be paid to Customs by you (difference between boxes 3 and 4)	Box 5	
Total value of sales and all other outputs excluding VAT (whole pounds only)	Box 6	
Total value of purchases and all other inputs excluding VAT (whole pounds only)	Box 7	
Total value of intra-community dispatches of goods and related costs, excluding VAT., from Northern Ireland to EU Member States	Box 8	
Total value of intra-community acquisitions of goods and related costs, excluding VAT, made in Northern Ireland from EU Member States	Box 9	

Chapter 11 – Answers

Task 1

Alexandra has given you the following list of sales made this month, but there are numbers missing. Complete the table below by working out the net, VAT or total amounts. All sales were made at the standard rate of 20%.

Note: Net amount before VAT = VAT exclusive of VAT
Gross amount after VAT – VAT inclusive of VAT

Invoice number:	Net amount (before VAT)	VAT	Gross amount (after VAT)
001	150.00	30.00	**180.00**
002	400.00	**80.00**	480.00
003	300.00	**60.00**	360.00
004	**260.00**	52.00	312.00
005	**700.00**	140.00	840.00
006	60.00	**12.00**	**72.00**
007	**1000.00**	200.00	**1200.00**
008	96.50	**19.30**	115.80
009	65.50	**13.10**	78.60
010	**55.80**	11.16	66.96

Task 2

a) Indicate whether the following statements are true or false.

	True	False
A taxable person is a business that is, or should be, registered for VAT.	√	
Output tax is always charged at 20% by a VAT registered business.		√
Reduced rate VAT is charged at 5%.	√	
A business who sells only exempt supplies are not making taxable supplies.	√	

b) Complete the missing figures in the table below.

Invoice number:	VAT rate	Net amount (before VAT)	VAT	Gross amount (after VAT)
AB1	20%	35.00	**7.00**	**42.00**
AB2	5%	26.00	1.30	**27.30**
AB3	20%	**98.50**	19.70	118.20
AB4	0%	86.00	**0.00**	**86.00**
AB5	5%	**66.00**	3.30	69.30
AB6	5%	**102.00**	5.10	**107.10**

Task 3

a) Carys started her business on 1 November 2021. Her monthly taxable turnover is £10,000 per month.

(i) What month does she exceed the current threshold of £85,000?

> Workings:
> £85,000 / £10,000 = 8.5 months
> Or running totals like this
> November - £10,000
> December - £20,000
> January - £30,000
> February - £40,000
> March - £50,000
> April - £60,000
> May - £70,000
> June - £80,000
> July - £90,000
>
> July was the month in which the threshold was exceeded.

Answer: ~~June~~ / **July** / ~~August~~ / ~~September~~

(ii) By what date should she notify HMRC?

Answer: **31 August 2022** / ~~31 July 2022~~ / ~~31 September 2021~~

(iii) When will her VAT registration start from?

Answer: ~~1 August 2022~~ / **1 September 2022** / 31 August 2022

b) Stacey is starting a new business on 1 May 2023 selling agricultural machinery and expects her turnover to be in the region of £250,000 a month. These are all taxable supplies.

What date does Stacey need to register from?

Answer: **1 May 2023** /~~31 May 2023 / 1 June 2023~~

c) Trudy started business on 1 April 2022. Her taxable turnover for the first 6 months was £6,000 a month, then it rose to £10,000 a month.

(i) On what date does Trudy's business exceed the threshold.

Workings:
**6 months (April – September 2022) x £6,000 = £36,000
Month 7 – October - £10,000, so total now £46,000
November – another £10,000, so total now £56,000
December – another £10,000, so total now £66,000
January – another £10,000, so total now £76,000
February – another £10,000, so total now £86,000**

The threshold was exceeded in February.

Answer: ~~December 2022 / January 2023~~ / **February 2023**

(ii) By what date should Trudy notify HMRC.

Answer: ~~31 January 2023 / 28 February 2023~~ / **31 March 2023**

Task 4

Identify the actual tax points in the following examples by ticking the correct box.

Sheena receives payment from a customer on 1 March. She dispatches the goods on 5 March. She issues the invoice on 17 March.	**1 March**	~~5 March~~	~~15 March~~
Ferhaan receives payment from a customer on 1 April. He dispatches the goods on 1 May. He issues the invoice on 5 May.	**1 April**	~~1 May~~	~~5 May~~
Kaye dispatches goods on 1 July. She issues the invoice on 12 July. She receives payment on 15 August.	~~1 July~~	**12 July**	~~15 August~~
Carly receives an order on 1 June. She dispatches the goods on 5 June. She issues the invoice on 6 June and receives payment the same day.	~~1 June~~	~~5 June~~	**6 June**
Zenildo issues an invoice to a customer on 2 June. He dispatches the goods on 4 June. He receives payment on 10 June.	**2 June**	~~4 June~~	~~10 June~~
Mo receives payment for goods on 1 October. He dispatches goods on 4 October. He issues the invoice on 6 October.	~~1 October~~	~~4 October~~	**6 October**

Explanations:
Sheena received the payment first and the invoice was not issued within 14 days.

Ferhaan received the payment first and the invoice was not issued within 14 days.

Kaye dispatched the goods on 1 July, but the invoice was issued within 14 days.

Carly received the order first, but this is irrelevant. The first thing that happened was the dispatch, but the invoice was issued within 14 days.

Zenildo issued the invoice first, so this is the tax point.

Mo received the payment first, but the invoice was issued within 14 days.

Task 5

a) Complete the following invoices.
   Hint: remember to round down the VAT.

Quantity	Unit price £	Total
400	3.50	**1,400.00**
100	1.27	**127.00**
50	0.60	**30.00**
	Total net price	**1,557.00**
	VAT at 20%	**311.40**
	Total invoice	**1,868.40**

Quantity	Unit price £	Total
27	1.21	**32.67**
33	1.59	**52.47**
49	2.11	**103.39**
	Total net price	**188.53**
	VAT at 20%	**37.70**
	Total invoice	**226.23**

b) Alicja issues an invoice for standard rated goods. The list price of the goods was £580 excluding VAT. She offers the customer a trade discount of 10%. How much VAT will be shown on the invoice?

Workings:
£580 less 10% = £522
[580 x 10% = 58. 580 - 58 = 522]
£522 x 20% = £104.40
If you have used a different method, but have the same answer, great.

Answer: **£104.40**

c) Baiba sells bookcases with a normal selling price of £240. She is running a sale at the moment where she is offering to pay the VAT for the customer. How much VAT will she need to show on her discounted invoice?

> Workings: **£240 includes VAT.**
> **(240/120) x 20 = £40 VAT**
> **The new sales price will be £240 less £40 = £200**
>
> **The new invoice will show:**
> **Net total £166.67 [200/120, then multiplied by 100 and rounded]**
> **VAT £33.33 [200/120, then multiplied by 20 and rounded down]**
> **Total invoice £200.00**

Answer: **£33.33**

d) True or false?

A business offers a prompt payment discount to its customers if they pay within 7 days. The invoice is sent for the full amount, and a credit note is sent for the discount allowed if the customer takes advantage of the discount and pays within the 7 days.

True / ~~False~~

Task 6

Calculate the amount of VAT that can be reclaimed on each of the following expenses for a VAT registered trader (business). Remember that some VAT is blocked.

	VAT inclusive amount £	VAT reclaimable £
A delivery van bought to deliver goods to customers.	33,600.00	**5,600.00**
A restaurant meal for a UK based customer to thank them for their custom.	264.00	**0.00** [this VAT is blocked]
A car purchased for use by the employees and kept on the work premises when not in use (pool car).	19,200.00	**3,200.00**
A Christmas party where the employees each bring a guest, meaning half are employees and half are not.	984.00	**82.00** [half the VAT can be reclaimed but the other half is blocked]
A hotel and meal for a customer visiting from China to discuss future work.	228.00	**38.00**
A car purchased for use by the director, with mixed personal and business use.	25,200.00	**0.00** [blocked because this is not solely for business use]
Stationery for use in the office at the head office.	105.60	**17.60**

Task 7

a) Cathy purchases a car for use in her business, which she intends to use for private journeys at the weekends.

(i) Can she reclaim VAT on the purchase cost of the vehicle?

~~YES~~ / **NO** because it is not solely for business use.

(ii) If Cathy pays the fuel scale charge, can she reclaim the VAT on the running costs of the car?

YES / ~~NO~~ because she is paying the charge to HMRC

b) Complete the table below to show whether output tax should be charged on the sale of the following non-current assets.

Non-current asset	Input tax reclaimed on original purchase	Sale price excluding VAT	Output tax to be charged on sale
Delivery van	Yes	13,500.00	**2,700.00**
Car	No	6,000.00	**0.00**
Machinery	Yes	14,000.00	**2,800.00**

Task 8

Trudy's business makes both taxable and exempt supplies (sales). She uses the partial exemption scheme to calculate the VAT she can reclaim on her purchases.

Trudy has provided you with the following information.

Taxable supplies for the quarter	£28,000
Exempt supplies for the quarter	£8,000

Input VAT for taxable supplies	£700
Input VAT for exempt supplies	£500
Input VAT for other expenses	£300

Calculate how much input tax can be reclaimed this quarter.

Workings:
Test 1: The total input tax is £1,500. £1,500 divided by the 3 months is £500. This is below the de miminus limit of £625 per month, so all the input tax can be reclaimed.
No need for test 2.

Answer: **£1,500**

Task 9

Stacey's business makes both taxable and exempt supplies. Details of the business activity for the past quarter is shown below.

Taxable supplies	£70,000
Exempt supplies	£20,000
Input tax on taxable supplies	£1,500
Input tax on exempt supplies	£1,500
Input tax on mixed overheads (expenses)	£1,500

Calculate the amount of input tax that can be reclaimed this quarter.

Workings:

Test 1: Total input tax is £4,500 [1,500 + 1,500 + 1,500]

£4,500 / 3 months = £1,500 per month which is above the de minimus limit.

Test 2: Input tax on taxable supplies is £1,500, which is £500 per month. This is below the de minimum limit. The exempt supplies are also less than 50% of the total sales. [20,000/70,000 = 28.5%.

As both the rules for the second test are satisfied, all the input tax can be reclaimed.

Answer: **£4,500**

Task 10

George operates the standard VAT scheme and submits his VAT returns quarterly. He has provided you with the following information.

	Net £	VAT £	Total £
SDB – standard rated sales	10,000	2,000	12,000
SDB – zero rated sales	5,000	0	5,000
PDB – standard rated purchases	4,000	800	4,800
PDB – zero rated purchases	200	0	200
PRDB – standard rated purchase returns	300	60	360

Complete the VAT return using this information. Be careful to include two decimal places in boxes 1 to 5, and whole pounds in boxes 6 to 9.

VAT Return 1 Jan 23 to 31 Mar 23		£
VAT due on sales and other outputs	Box 1	**2,000.00**
VAT due on intra-community acquisitions of goods made in Northern Ireland from EU member states	Box 2	**0.00**
Total VAT due (the sum of boxes 1 and 2)	Box 3	**2,000.00**
VAT reclaimed on purchases and other inputs (including acquisitions from the EU)	Box 4	**740.00**
Net VAT to be paid to Customs by you (difference between boxes 3 and 4)	Box 5	**1,260.00**
Total value of sales and all other outputs excluding VAT (whole pounds only)	Box 6	**15,000**
Total value of purchases and all other inputs excluding VAT (whole pounds only)	Box 7	**3,900**
Total value of intra-community dispatches of goods and related costs, excluding VAT., from Northern Ireland to EU Member States	Box 8	**0**
Total value of intra-community acquisitions of goods and related costs, excluding VAT, made in Northern Ireland from EU Member States	Box 9	**0**

Note that the purchase returns are deducted from the purchases and the VAT on purchase returns is deducted from the VAT on purchases.

Task 11

a) Khan Systems is a small business making only taxable supplies. They have provided you with the following information.

Standard rated sales including VAT	£44,004
Standard rated sales returns including VAT	£3,000
Standard rated purchases including VAT	£12,000
Standard rated purchase returns including VAT	£600
Zero rated purchases	£2,000

Calculate the VAT payable or reclaimable for Khan Systems.

Workings:
(44,004 / 120) x 20 = 7,334 – VAT on sales
(3,000 / 120) x 20 = 500 – VAT on sales returns
So total payable to HMRC is £6,834

(12,000 / 120) x 20 = 2,000 – VAT on purchases
(600 / 120) x 20 = 100 – VAT on purchase returns
So total reclaimable from HMRC is £1,900

£6,834 - £1,900 = £4,934 payable

Answer: **£4,934** **payable**/reclaimable

b) Prime Ltd has output tax this quarter of £18,000 and input tax of £22,000. Calculate the amount payable to or reclaimable from HMRC.

Answer: **£4,000 reclaimable [the input tax is higher than the output tax so this will be reclaimed from HMRC).**

Task 12

a) Jenny has written off a bad debt in her accounts that is more than 6 months old. The customer owed £3,600 including VAT. Calculate the amount of VAT Jenny can claim as bad debt relief and identify which box she needs to add this to.

Bad debt relief: **£600 [(3,600 / 120) x 20]**

Add to Box: **4**

b) Jenny has provided you with information about a net error in her previous VAT return, which was neither careless or deliberate. Identify whether she can include this in her next VAT return or whether she has to make a separate disclosure.

Net error is £11,000
Turnover for the period (box 6 figure) is £90,000

Answer: ~~Include in next VAT return~~ / *make a separate disclosure.*-[over 10,000, and more than 1% of the turnover]

c) Regan is completing his VAT return for the quarter and has discovered the following errors in the previous VAT return. All were non-deliberate and non-careless.

The input tax was under-stated by £300.
No input tax was claimed on the purchase of a new machine costing £18,000 including VAT.
Input tax was wrongly claimed on the purchase of a car costing £33,180 including VAT.

Identify the net error and decide whether this can be included in the VAT return or whether a separate disclosure is needed.

> Workings: **Input tax understated by £300 – reclaimable from HMRC.**
> £18,000 inc VAT, so (18,000 / 120) x 20 = £3,000 reclaimable from HMRC
> £33,180 inc VAT, so (12,000 / 120) x 20 = £5,530 owed to HMRC as this should not have been claimed last time.
> £300 to reclaim
> £3,000 to reclaim
> £5,530 owed
> **Total to pay HMRC is £2,230**

Net error amount: **£2,230**

Enter in next VAT return /~~Separate disclosure required~~ **below £10,000**

Task 13

Identify whether the following statements are true or false.

Statement	True	False
An employee can register for payroll up to 6 months before they pay their first employee.		√
Payroll records must be kept for a minimum of 2 years.		√
Income tax (PAYE) is a statutory deduction.	√	
Income tax (PAYE) is calculated on net pay.		√
A charitable donation is an example of a non-statutory deduction.	√	
Gross pay, minus deductions equals net pay.	√	

Task 14

a) RTI is the system which requires all employers to submit their payroll information to HMRC. What does RTI stand for?

Answer: **Real Time Information**

b) FPS is a report submitted by all employers on or before the pay date giving information about the payments made to, and deduction made from, employees. What does FPS stand for?

Answer: **Full payment submission**

c) If an employer has not paid any employees during the month, which report must be submitted to HMRC declaring this? Choose the correct option.

~~FPS / P45 / RTI~~ / **EPS** / ~~P11D~~

d) When an employee leaves, the employer must issue them with which of the following? Choose the correct option.

~~P60~~ / **P45** / ~~P11D~~

e) Identify whether the following statements are true or false.

Statement	True	False
A P60 contains information about the employee benefits for the year, such as company car.		√
An employer does not need to issue a payslip if the gross pay is less than £150.		√
The employer will pay NIC class 1a on taxable benefits provided to employees.	√	
PAYE and NIC deductions must be paid to HMRC by the 22nd of the following month if payments are made electronically.	√	

Task 15

a) Ollie makes only exempt supplies. His turnover was £90,000 for the past 12 months. Does he need to register for VAT?

~~Yes /~~ **No (because he makes only exempt supplies)**

b) Roger makes only zero-rated supplies. His turnover was £90,000 for the past 12 months. Does he need to register for VAT?

Yes / ~~No~~ **(because he makes taxable supplies that have exceeded the threshold)**

c) Rusty makes both standard and zero rates supplies. His standard rated supplies for the past 12 months totalled £50,000. His zero-rated supplies for the past 12 months totalled £40,000. Does he need to register for VAT.

Yes / ~~No~~ **(because all his supplies are taxable supplies and these together have exceeded the threshold)**

d) Mary makes both standard rated and exempt supplies. Her standard rated supplies for the past 12 months totalled £40,000. Her exempt supplies for the past 12 months totalled £90,000. Does she need to register for VAT?

~~Yes /~~ **No (because her taxable supplies are only £40,000)**

Task 16

a) Carys delivers goods to a customer on 2 April 2023. She issues the invoice on 10 April 2023. The customer pays on 15 April 2023.

What is the tax point?

~~2 April~~ / **10 April** / ~~15 April~~ **(because the delivery date was the basic tax point, but the invoice was issued within 14 days of this, so the 14-day rule applies.**

b) Identify whether input tax can be reclaimed on the following purchases/expenses.

Purchase / expense	Reclaimable	Not reclaimable
A car purchased for use as a taxi.	√	
Food for the Christmas party for employees only.	√	
A car purchased for use by the director for both business and private journeys.		√
Cost of entertaining customers visiting from China.	√	
Cost of entertaining UK customers at local restaurant.		√
A van purchased for use within the business.	√	

c) Jane has decided to pay the fuel scale charge to reclaim VAT on the running costs of the director's car. The amount payable is £240. To which box of the VAT should this charge be added?

> Answer: **Box 1 (because this is the amount payable to HMRC and this is a charge that she must pay)**

d) Jane wishes to claim bad debt relief on two irrecoverable debts. She has provided you with the following information. Identify which VAT period the bad debt relief can be claimed and calculate the amount to be reclaimed. Choose the correct option.

Bad debt inc VAT £	Date payment was due	VAT period in which the bad debt relief can be claimed	Amount of bad debt relief to be reclaimed £
3,600	30 Aug 2022	**Quarter ending 31 Mar 2023** ~~Quarter ending 30 Jun 2023~~ ~~Quarter ending 30 Sept 2023~~	**600**
540	30 Nov 2022	~~Quarter ending 31 Mar 2023~~ **Quarter ending 30 Jun 2023** ~~Quarter ending 30 Sept 2023~~	**90**
1,200	31 Dec 2022	~~Quarter ending 31 Mar 2023~~ **Quarter ending 30 Jun 2023** ~~Quarter ending 30 Sept 2023~~	**200**

Task 17

Complete the following table by filling in the missing figures.

Net amount £	VAT rate	VAT amount £	Total £
200.00	20%	40.00	240.00
310.00	5%	**15.50**	325.50
1,470.00	20%	294.00	1764.00
387.25	20%	**77.45**	**464.70**
474.63	5%	**23.73**	**498.36**
2,680.80	0%	0.00	2680.80
9,761.33	20%	**1,952.26**	**11,713.59**
7,330.00	20%	1,466.00	**8,796.00**
2,600.00	5%	130.00	**2,730.00**

Task 18

Heron Enterprises has calculated the VAT owed to HMRC this quarter as £3,185.95.

It has been noticed that a credit note sent to a supplier for goods returned has not been included in the records. The credit note was for £250 plus VAT.

a) Calculate the VAT amount on the credit note.

Answer: **£50**

b) Calculate the adjusted amount payable to HMRC.

Answer: **£3,135.95 [3,185.95 – 50 as this is no longer payable to HMRC because it reduces the amount payable]**

c) The amount payable to HMRC is shown in which box of the VAT return?

Answer: Box **5**

Task 19

Monika started her business on 1 April 2022. She makes only standard rated supplies. Her taxable supplies are approximately £15,000 every month.

a) In which month will Monika exceed the threshold for registration?

Workings:
April £15,000, running total £15,000.
May £15,000, running total £30,000
June £15,000, running total £45,000
July £15,000, running total £60,000
August £15,000, running total £75,000
September £15,000, running total £90,000 – above the threshold

Answer: **September 2022**

b) By what date does Monika need to notify HMRC that she has exceeded the threshold?

Answer: **31 October 2022 (30 days after the month the threshold was reached)**

c) What date will Monika need to start accounting for VAT?

Answer: **1 November 2022**

Task 20

a) Richard runs a market stall selling fresh vegetables. All his sales are zero-rated, and his turnover is well below the compulsory registration threshold. He chooses to register for VAT. Which of the following might be his reason for voluntarily registering for VAT?

~~a. He can start charging VAT on his sales.~~
~~b. He makes only zero-rated purchases.~~
c. He makes a mix of zero and standard rated purchases. (He can claim back the VAT on the standard rated purchases).

b) George runs a market stall selling fresh fish. All his sales are zero-rated but his turnover is above the compulsory registration threshold. He has applied to be exempt from registration. Which of the following might be his reason for applying for exemption?

a. His business makes only zero-rated purchases. (He would have nothing to pay HMRC and nothing to claim back as his purchases are also zero-rated).
~~b. He doesn't want to charge VAT to his customers.~~
~~c. His prices will need to increase if he registers.~~

c) True or false?

If a business makes a mix of standard rated and exempt supplies, it cannot claim back any input tax?

~~True~~ / **False (They can claim some of the input tax, or all of the input tax if they meet the de minimus conditions).**

Task 21

Lang is completing her VAT return for the quarter. She has provided you with the following information, taking from the VAT account.

Output tax   £42,000
Input tax   £14,000

You are also told that no adjustments have been made for the following.

Bad debt relief on an invoice totalling £360.00 including VAT.
Fuel scale charges with a total VAT of £140.

a) What will the entry be for Box 1 of the VAT return?

Workings: **42,000 output tax + fuel scale charge 140 = 42,140**

Answer: **£42,140**

b) What will the entry be for Box 4 of the VAT return?

Workings: **14,000 + 60 [(360/120)x20) = 14,060**

Answer: **£14,060**

c) How much VAT is payable due to, or from HMRC?

Answer: **£28,080- [£42,140-£14,060]**

Task 22

Identify whether the following statements are true or false.

Statement	True	False
The amount of pay an employee receives after deductions is called the net pay.	√	
An employer must register for payroll before the first pay day.	√	
Mavis employs one part-time employee, but she is a sole trader, so she does not have to register for payroll.		√
Net pay = gross pay – employee's NI contribution – income tax.	√	
Income tax and NICs are compulsory deductions from an employee's pay.	√	
Employers can send payslips to employees in paper-format only.		√
An EPS report is used if the employer has paid employees during the month.		√
A P45 is issued by the employer to an employee who is leaving their employment.	√	
The P11D is completed by an employer for every employee who has received taxable benefits during the year.	√	
A P60 is given to all employees every time they are paid.		√
A tax month for payroll is from the 1st to the 30th or 31st of the month.		√

Task 23

Identify whether the following errors can be declared in the next VAT return or whether they need to be separately disclosed to HMRC.

Amount of error £	Turnover for the current period £	Include in next VAT return	Separate disclosure required
4,000	80,000	√	
14,000	150,000		√
52,000	1,500,000		√
300	30,000	√	
8,000	80,000	√	
28,000	3,000,000	√	
1,000	50,000	√	
13,000	90,000		√
12,000	1,300,000	√	
60,000	32,000,000		√

Explanations:

If the error is below £10,000 it can always be included in the next VAT return.

If the error is between £10,000 and £50,000 it can be included in the next VAT return so long as the error is less than 1% of the turnover.

If the error is above £50,000 it must always be separately disclosed.

Task 24

Justine receives a deposit from a customer on 8 July 2022.

She dispatches the goods on 20 July 2022.

She sends the invoice on 25 July 2022.

She receives the balance of the payment on 28 July 2022.

a) Identify the tax point for the deposit.

Answer: **8 July 2022 (the payment for the deposit is received first, so this has its own tax point).**

b) Identify the tax point for the balance of the invoice.

Answer: **25 July 2022 (the deposit has already been dealt with, so the next date is the dispatch date, but the invoice is issued within 14 days of the dispatch date, so the 14-day rule applies, and the invoice date can be used)**

Task 25

Shirley is a VAT registered trader. She has provided you with the following information for her VAT return for the quarter ending 31 March 2023.

	Net £	VAT £	Total £
SDB – standard rated sales	47,000.00	9,400.00	56,400.00
SRDB – standard rated sales returns	3,000.00	600.00	3,600.00
PDB – standard rated purchases	12,500.00	2,500.00	15,000.00
PDB – zero rated purchases	800.00	0.00	800.00
PRDB – standard rated purchase returns	600.00	120.00	720.00

You have also been told the following:

A car was purchased for £30,000 including VAT and no entries have been made for this.

An adjustment needs to be made for a bad debt of £4,800 including VAT.

Complete the VAT return on the next page using this information.

Workings: **Box 1 – sales VAT 9,400 less sales returns VAT 600 = 8,800**
Box 2 – zero
Box 3 – 1 and 2 together = 8,800
Box 4 – purchases VAT 2,500 – purchase returns VAT 120 = 1,380 + the VAT on the bad debt to reclaim of 800 = 3,180
Box 5 – box 3 less box 4 = 5,620
Box 6 – total sales 47,000 – sales returns 3,000 = 44,000
Box 7 – total purchases 12,500 + 800 – purchase returns 600 = 12,700 – car purchase of £30,000 (no VAT to reclaim on the car) = £42,700
Boxes 8 and 9 are both 0.

VAT Return 1 Jan 23 to 31 Mar 23		£
VAT due on sales and other outputs	Box 1	**8,800.00**
VAT due on intra-community acquisitions of goods made in Northern Ireland from EU member states	Box 2	**0.00**
Total VAT due (the sum of boxes 1 and 2)	Box 3	**8,800.00**
VAT reclaimed on purchases and other inputs (including acquisitions from the EU)	Box 4	**3,180.00**
Net VAT to be paid to Customs by you (difference between boxes 3 and 4)	Box 5	**5,620.00**
Total value of sales and all other outputs excluding VAT (whole pounds only)	Box 6	**44,000**
Total value of purchases and all other inputs excluding VAT (whole pounds only)	Box 7	**42,700**
Total value of intra-community dispatches of goods and related costs, excluding VAT., from Northern Ireland to EU Member States	Box 8	**0**
Total value of intra-community acquisitions of goods and related costs, excluding VAT, made in Northern Ireland from EU Member States	Box 9	**0**

If you have enjoyed this workbook, you might like to try more of my books. They are all available from Amazon in both paperback and as eBooks. The links to my workbooks can be found here. https://www.teresaclarke.co.uk/

Teresa Clarke FMAAT

Printed in Great Britain
by Amazon